THE ONE-YEAR NOVELIST

A WEEK-BY-WEEK GUIDE TO WRITING YOUR NOVEL IN ONE YEAR

L. M. LILLY

INTRODUCTION

If you're like me, and like most writers, you can't devote every waking hour to writing a novel. You need to fit it in along with other responsibilities.

You might be raising children, working another full-time (or more than full-time) job, pursuing a degree, or all of the above.

Because of that, writing and finishing a novel can feel overwhelming. And when you hear about those authors who publish a book a month—forget it.

The good news is that you can start with an idea and finish a solid draft—one you're

Introduction

comfortable sharing with an editor or beta readers— within one year by following the week-by-week plan in this book.

This plan works whether you're able to follow the age-old advice of writing the same time every week or day or whether your schedule varies widely from week to week and month to month.

It's designed to work around a full-time or more than full-time career or job, a family, and/or other demands on your time.

In fact, the weekly breakdown assumes you don't have endless hours—or perhaps a single hour at any one time—to hide away and do nothing but write.

For the same reason, the weekly breakdown allows for times when you might speed ahead and others when you need to set your novel aside for a while. You can also feel free to shift tasks to different days that work better for you during a given week.

Getting Started

You can start your one year, and your novel, any time.

Introduction

The weeks are numbered. Whether you begin January 1, November 1, or April 15 (but maybe don't start then if you're in the United States, as tax time is already stressful enough), it's Week 1.

Follow the steps and you'll finish in Week 52.

What This Book Includes (And Doesn't)

The week-by-week plan briefly covers plot turns and character development because knowing your story's major turns and your main characters ahead of time eliminates figuring everything out on the fly, which slows the writing process. An overview of point of view and viewpoint characters is included as well.

These topics aren't discussed in depth, though, because delving into each would make **The One-Year Novelist** more of a writing guide and less of a one-year plan.

Many weeks in the following pages also include ways to strengthen your commitment to finishing your novel in a year.

Introduction

That's important because without commitment, when there's an open twenty minutes in your schedule you're more apt to think something like:

- *Twenty minutes isn't enough to get anything written*
- *It'll take me that long to find my place again and get rolling*
- *The kids really want a ride to their friends' house*
- *I haven't cleaned the kitchen in a week*

Some of these are real issues. At some point you need to clean the kitchen, and your children (or other family members and friends) do need you.

But we were talking about twenty minutes that weren't spoken for yet, so these questions are about wanting to write a novel, but not being committed enough yet to doing it. If you're committed, you'll seize those twenty minutes to write.

Happily, you've already made a commitment by reading this book, and the weekly breakdown includes steps to help you stick with it.

Introduction

What If You're Not A Planner (Or You've Already Outlined Your Novel)

If you're not a planner, don't worry, the week-by-week process doesn't require a detailed outline that will keep you from exploring as you write.

If you'd like to skip the planning phase, though, either because you prefer to do all your exploring as you write or you've already outlined or sketched out your novel, you can use **The One-Year Novelist** with a few changes.

Read through the planning weeks in one shot. (It'll be quick, as that's only 11 pages with lots of white space.)

Do the commitment exercises in Weeks 1, 3, and 6. This will take 15-30 minutes tops.

Start with Week 12 and keep pace with the word count goals.

When you hit a week that refers to a plot turn covered in Weeks 1-8, you can do one of two things:

(1) Reread that week and see if or how it ap-

Introduction

plies to your writing. If you need to, take an extra week to work through that. (You've got 11 weeks to spare!)

(2) Write straight through without pausing or being concerned about your plot turns, staying within the word count goals for each week. At the end, you can use the extra 11 weeks to adjust your plot if you find you need it.

Either way, you'll have a solid first draft at the end of the year.

My Story

Because I'm sharing a one-year plan for writing novels, you may want to know what I've written.

At every stage of my adult life I've written and finished novels. I finished my first one (not published) while working at my first full-time job. That job was basically 9-5, making it pretty easy to keep to the same writing schedule every week.

I wrote other novels while temping, so I'd work a few weeks when I really needed money, then take time off to write.

Introduction

Of the 4 books in my Awakening supernatural thriller series, all but the last one (The Illumination) were written when I was practicing law anywhere from 40-65 hours a week, and I almost never worked the same hours from week to week. Each novel took less time to write as I adjusted my schedule and made better use of my time.

There were months, though, that I wrote no fiction at all and others when I left my office every day around 6 p.m. and was able to fit in 2-3 hours of fiction writing a week.

Now, although I spend fewer hours at law, I still juggle multiple responsibilities, including teaching legal writing, running the website WritingAsASecondCareer.com, hosting the podcast Buffy and the Art of Story (a podcast for writers who love Buffy the Vampire Slayer) and writing non-fiction. All of which means my schedule still varies widely from week to week and month to month.

In short, the advice to write the same time every day or week has almost never been feasible for me. I suspect it's not for many peo-

Introduction

ple, which is another reason I wrote **The One-Year Novelist**.

My first published novel, **The Awakening**, has been downloaded over 70,000 times and reached No. 1 in numerous categories for free and paid books on Amazon, including Occult, Horror, Feminist, and Paranormal. The second book in my Q.C. Davis mystery series, The Charming Man, was recently named a finalist in the 2019 Wishing Shelf Book Awards.

I hope this history shows that despite other demands on your time, you can still write and finish your novel.

Tracking Your Progress

If you're like me and want to write or type notes on whatever you figure out about your novel and track your word count, you can write in the workbook edition of this book or use this free downloadable template.

Spoilers

Throughout this book, I use examples from **Pride and Prejudice** by Jane Austen. I chose it because many people are familiar with the

Introduction

story in the form of the book, film(s), and the mini-series.

If you haven't read or seen it, I include enough context for you to understand the examples. But be warned—I give away major plot turns, though not the ending. So now's the time to watch it or read it if you don't want anything spoiled.

Okay, are you ready to start—and finish—your novel?

Read on for Week 1.

PART ONE: FROM IDEA TO PLOT

1

WEEK 1

Days 1-2
Commitment

- Tell 3 people that you will finish your novel by this time next year.

Ask each one if you can check in (via email, text, or some other type of message) every 4 weeks from now until then to share an update on your progress.

They don't need to respond if they don't want to.

(Don't rely on social media. Commitments are harder to break if they are made to specific people.)

Days 3-4

Conflict And The Protagonist's Goal

Without a conflict, there's no story. (If you don't believe it, think of every novel, film, TV series, or play you've ever loved. Each one centered around a conflict.)

The best way to create a strong conflict is for your main character to want something that is hard to achieve.

Answer these 3 questions about your protagonist's goal:

- What does your main character (your protagonist) want?
- What makes it hard to achieve?
- Why does your protagonist desperately want or need to achieve this goal?

Days 5-7

More About Your Protagonist

- Write two paragraphs about your protagonist.

If you're not sure where to start, ask yourself what's most important about that character. Why do you want to write about her/him/it? How do factors such as the protagonist's age, gender, ethnicity, cultural background, job, education, family, or friends affect the story?

2
WEEK 2

Days 1-5
The Antagonist

For the strongest conflict, your antagonist's goal should be in direct conflict with the protagonist's goal such that only one can win. In other words, if the protagonist achieves her goal, the antagonist fails to achieve hers and vice versa.

- Write down your antagonist's goal.
- Write two paragraphs about why the antagonist needs or desperately wants to achieve this goal.
- Write two more paragraphs about

your antagonist, highlighting the antagonist's strengths and what makes him/her/it a strong foe for the protagonist.

Days 6-7

Character Beliefs

Understanding your characters' global beliefs (meaning beliefs that affect all areas of life) will help you write a richer novel and develop a stronger plot.

- Brainstorm 3 global beliefs that your protagonist holds.

For instance, does he believe people are generally good (or bad)?

That she is the only one she can truly count on when it comes down to it?

That rich people are evil or poor people just need to pull themselves up by their boot straps?

- Do the same thing for your antagonist.

3
WEEK 3

Days 1-2
Commitment

- Write at least a paragraph about why you want to write and finish a novel.

For example, will you be proud of yourself? Will you be fulfilling a lifelong dream? Do you look forward to telling your friend or spouse or boss you've done it? Do you hope to make a living writing novels?

Days 3-4

Character Values

Your characters' values also will drive them and the story.

Values can heighten conflict without the need to rely on black-and-white good vs. evil characterizations (though those can be fun too).

For example, in a romance or a family drama you might have a protagonist who highly values peace and getting along with others, and an antagonist who believes that arguing every point is the best way to foster an honest, authentic relationship.

Or a protagonist might believe a single strong leader is needed to get the best work from a team while the antagonist believes too much power should never be concentrated in the same hands.

These differences create conflict no matter what type of novel you're writing.

- What do your protagonist and antagonist value most highly?
- Does that create conflict?

- If not, brainstorm other or additional values.

Days 5-7

More Conflict

- If the antagonist's and the protagonist's goals are not mutually exclusive (meaning it's impossible for both to prevail), revise one or both goals so that they are.
- Think of 3 ways you can make it harder for your protagonist to reach her goal.

4
WEEK 4

Days 1-2
Commitment

- Check in with your 3 people.

No need to provide details.

Write something like: *Figured out main conflict and characters. Right on track!*

Days 3-6

The Story Spark

The Story Spark, or Inciting Incident, gets the ball rolling. It usually happens on your first page or in the first chapter.

The classic example is a murder mystery, where the dead body is found. Without it, there's no story, and no conflict for our protagonist.

- Think about your protagonist's main goal, the one that will take the entire novel to reach (or to clearly fail to reach).
- When is the first time something significant happens that makes your protagonist start moving toward that goal? Or that blocks that goal?
- Write that down – it's your Story Spark.

Day 7

Rest.

5
WEEK 5

Days 1-6
The One-Quarter Twist

A fourth of the way through your novel, an event needs to occur that raises the stakes and spins the plot in a new direction.

This event comes from outside the protagonist.

In **Pride and Prejudice,** the protagonist, Elizabeth Bennett, attends a ball where nearly all her family members embarass themselves to a very great degree, though none of them realize it. This display appalls the antagonist (Darcy). It also spins the story in a new direction because Darcy's best friend, Bingley, and Elizabeth's oldest sister have fallen in love. Darcy decides to do all he can to separate the two. Suddenly, Bingley leaves town. Elizabeth is devastated for her sister, and when she later learns of Darcy's role in her sister's heartbreak, she believes him to be the worst of men.

- Think about turns your story could take that force your protagonist to change course or alter how she is dealing with the conflict we saw in the Story Spark.
- Write the phrase "What If...." and come up with as many options as you can for how your story might turn at the quarter point. Ideally, list 15 or 20.
- Circle (or highlight) the strongest 5 What Ifs.
- For each one, think about and/or write down how your protagonist's approach will change after each.
- Choose the one that creates the

most conflict or which resonates the most with you as your One-Quarter Twist.

Day 7

Rest.

WEEK 6

Day 1
Commitment

You've reached the halfway mark of your planning phase, and you're nearly ready to start writing.

If you're behind, don't worry, you'll catch up in later weeks.

- Plan what you'll do as a reward when you finish your novel. Write it down.

Days 2-7

The Mid-Point (also about commitment)

Many writers stall in their first draft about halfway through, struggling with the "saggy middle." That's why you'll spend these days planning a strong Mid-Point.

Until now, the protagonist has acted mainly in response to the Story Spark and the One-Quarter Twist.

At the Mid-Point all that changes. The protagonist commits with a capital C, throwing caution to the wind, often after suffering a serious reversal of fortune.

In **Pride and Prejudice**, Elizabeth rejects a marriage proposal from Darcy, telling him in no uncertain terms that she blames him for her sister's unhappiness and believes him to be a horrible person. This is no light matter, as Elizabeth and her sisters will be in desperate financial straits if none of them marry well. Eventually they will lose their home due to the way their father's estate is entailed, and none are married or have any prospects. Finally, though she doesn't know it, Elizabeth is wrong about a major part of

Darcy's conduct and will later realize she loves him.

Talk about throwing caution to the wind.

Darcy also throws caution to the wind. He gives Elizabeth a letter explaining his actions and revealing very personal and dangerous information about his own sister.

These scenes occur at the Mid-Point of the book and drive the rest of the story. Both grow from the One-Quarter Twist because that is what prompted Darcy to interfere in Elizabeth's sister's romance, incurring Elizabeth's anger.

- Think about possible Mid-Points that grow out of your One-Quarter Twist.
- How can your protagonist commit to a cause, a fight, or a larger goal?
- What's the throw-caution-to-the-wind moment?

7
WEEK 7

Days 1-6
The Three-Quarter Turn

The turn at the three-quarter point of your novel takes the story in a new and often unexpected direction. Unlike the twist at the one-quarter point, the Three-Quarter Turn arises directly from the protagonist's commitment at the Mid-Point.

In **Pride and Prejudice,** after receiving a distressing letter, Elizabeth reveals to Darcy that her youngest sister has run away with Wickham, a man whom Darcy despises. Before this, Elizabeth and Darcy appeared on the verge of commencing their own romance, both having altered their views of and approach to one another.

This complication turns the story.

Elizabeth is certain this proof of her sister's bad character (yes, sadly, that was how people thought then) and her alliance with Wickham will drive Darcy away. And it appears that it does. The family strives to find Wickham and force a marriage. Darcy's choices, and Elizabeth's, from this point on focus on this pursuit and its consequences and drive the story toward the Climax.

- Brainstorm at least 5 possible Three-Quarter Turns.

These should be major complications that logically arise from your protagonist's commitment at the Mid-Point and that significantly turn the plot.

- Write down how and why each one complicates the protagonist's life, what the protagonist does in response, and how the antagonist

uses the situation to drive toward the opposing goal.
- Choose the one that makes the protagonist's life the hardest and/or that works best for your story.

Day 7

Rest.

8
WEEK 8

Days 1-2
Commitment

- Check in with your 3 people.

If you're behind where you'd hoped to be, don't write the reasons or send them to your people. It'll only make you feel more behind.

Instead, look through the assignments for the upcoming weeks and share with them the week by which you expect to be back on track.

Days 3-5

Climax

- Figure out, if you don't already know, the payoff for your story.

One way or another, the central conflict of the book must end. The protagonist may out-and-out win, may be defeated utterly, may win partially, or may win but at such a cost it leaves him devastated (known as a pyrrhic victory).

Which do you choose?

- Write a paragraph summarizing what happens.

Days 6-7

The Rest Of The Story (The Falling Action)

- Note any loose ends you'll need to tie up after the Climax.

Include questions that will need answers and possibly (or definitely if you're planning a sequel) hints about the future.

WEEK 9

Days 1-7
Take A Break

- Don't write, don't plot, and don't think about your novel if you can help it.
- If you are behind, you can use this week to catch up, but try to give yourself at least a couple days away from your story.

WEEK 10

Days 1-3
Revisit

Though you took a break, your unconscious was working on your story.

- Review your Story Spark, One-Quarter Twist, Mid-Point, Three-Quarter Turn, and Climax.
- If there's anything you want to change, go ahead and do that.

Days 4-6

Characters

- Think about your characters, including the side characters you'll need to flesh out the story.
- Write a few paragraphs on each one who significantly affects your plot.

Day 7

Rest.

11

WEEK 11

Days 1-2
Commitment

A week from now you'll start writing your first draft!

- Write down what you'll enjoy most about writing it.

It might be immersing yourself in your fictional world, getting to know your characters better, sitting in a café and enjoying your favorite coffee (or tea or wine if you're like me) as you type away.

- Share these thoughts with a friend.

Days 3-7

Subplots

Most, though not all, novels have a subplot and possibly more than one. Subplots are secondary storylines that are usually less complex than the main plot.

- Think about your possible subplots.

If your main plot is in good shape, you can comfortably experiment with subplot(s) without needing to revamp your entire book. For that reason, you may want to simply let your subplots develop as you write rather than planning them.

- If you want to organize your subplots in advance, sketch out a possible Story Spark, Mid-Point, and Climax for each.

WEEK 12

Days 1-2
Commitment

- Check in with your 3 people.

(You're still updating them, right? If not, now's the time to get back in touch.)

Days 3-5

Point of View (Overall)

Before you start writing, you need to decide what overall point of view you'll use. Your options:

- **Third person omniscient** (narrator knows all)
- **Third person limited shifting** (multiple characters, third-person pronouns like "he" or "she" but each character stays within own knowledge)
- **Third person limited** (single character, "he" or "she," stays within single character's knowledge for entire novel)
- **Second person** (single character, second-person pronoun "you," stays within single character's knowledge for entire novel)
- **First person** (single character, first-person pronouns "I" and "me," stays within single character's knowledge for entire novel)

If you want to show your readers scenes — and provide information — that is solely within one character's knowledge or experience and from that character's perspective, you can choose any of the above. Otherwise, choose one of the third-person options so you can use multiple viewpoints.

- What point of view did you choose?

Days 6-7

Choose Viewpoint Character(s)

The best viewpoint character is almost always the character with the most at stake.

- What character (or characters) has the most at stake in your story?
- Decide on one or more viewpoint characters for your first draft. (You can adjust later if you need to.)

PART TWO: WRITING FROM POINT TO POINT

Congratulations!

You're ready to write.

For each week, a word count goal is listed. This breakdown assumes an average-length novel of 80,000 words.

To finish on time, you'll only need to write about 1 single-spaced page a day for 5 days out of 7. (Page length based on 12-point Times New Roman font.)

Also, you'll have 4 weeks that are set aside for breaks or to catch up on word count over the next 34 weeks.

If you can write exactly a page a day for 5 days every week, that's great, and you can follow the daily word count exactly.

If some days you have more time than others, you may write 5 or 6 pages on one day and none on another, so focus on the weekly word count goal.

If your schedule varies widely, aim to hit the word count goal every 4 weeks.

While your word processor will track word count for you, I like to actually write (yes, with a pen) my word count by day's end on a piece of paper on my wall. It helps me stay on track, especially when my word count varies from day to day.

If you hit a major snag, revisit your 5 points (the Story Spark, One-Quarter Twist, Mid-Point, Three-Quarter Turn, and Climax) and rework them. My advice, though, is to make a few notes on what you'll change and keep moving forward with the writing as if you'd already revised.

Writing without going back over previous pages will keep you on track. You can change the earlier part of the draft during the weeks toward the end of the process.

Similarly, if you realize you need to shift point of view or your viewpoint character(s), rather than revising right away make a note and move forward as if you'd already corrected the earlier pages.

This approach helps you finish on time.

It also ensures you don't spend many weeks rewriting only to find as you get further in the novel that your original version really was the best choice after all.

13

WEEK 13

Days 1-7
In The Beginning

- Average 533 words per day for at least 5 days.

Start with whatever scenes absolutely need to occur to set the stage and lead into the Story Spark. (See Part 1 Week 4 for more on the Story Spark.)

The Story Spark should occur in these pages or in the pages you'll write over the next 2 weeks.

- End of week word count: 2,665.

WEEK 14

Days 1-7
Moving Toward The Story Spark

- Average 533 words per day for at least 5 days.

If your Story Spark hasn't happened yet, you may be starting your story too early—before the real conflict begins. Skip some scenes if necessary to fit it in soon. (You might discover you don't need them.)

- End of week word count: 5,330.

WEEK 15

Days 1-2
Character Development

If there's a character you're trying to flesh out, think about how the character would behave on a half-hour coffee date with a stranger with whom the character hopes to later have a personal relationship.

- What three things would your character make a point to say?

These will be things the character believes will help make a good impression or believes the other person needs to know.

- What three things would your character almost certainly mention without consciously meaning to do so?

Here, we're not looking for things the character would purposely bring up but those that always seem to creep into that person's conversations, even with strangers.

Finally, most of us also know there are things we shouldn't say during a first meeting, and we intentionally hold back until we know a person better.

- What three things would your character take care not to do or say on a first meeting?

Days 3-7

Almost 10% Finished

- Average 533 words per day for at least 5 days.

You're almost 10% finished!

Your Story Spark should occur by the end of this week.

- End of week word count: 7,995.

WEEK 16

Day 1
Commitment

- Check in with your 3 people. Let them know where you're at and where you hope to be by Week 20, which is the next time you'll message them.

If you're a little behind right now, that's okay. There's a catch up week next week.

If you're ahead, think of it as banking some writing for when you hit a really busy time.

Days 2-7

Writing

- Average 533 words per day for at least 5 days.
- End of week word count: 10,660.

17

WEEK 17

Days 1-7
Catch Your Breath/Catch Up

We've covered a lot of ground over the last 16 weeks.

- If you're on schedule, take this week to:

1. Think about your upcoming One-Quarter Twist (See Part 1 Week 5 for more on the One-Quarter Twist)
2. Make notes on points you think you might want to adjust and/or
3. Rest!

- If you're behind, take this week to catch up.
- End of week word count: 10,660 (same as last week).

WEEK 18

Days 1-7
Writing And Subplots

- Average 533 words per day for at least 5 days.

If you haven't introduced your subplot(s) yet, now is a good time to start working that in. (See Part 1 Week 11 for more on subplots.)

- End of week word count: 13,325.

WEEK 19

Days 1-7
Writing – Nearing 25% Finished!

- Average 533 words per day for at least 5 days.

It's hard to believe, but in 2 weeks you'll have finished one quarter of your first draft.

- Think about other scenes you need to get to the One-Quarter Twist.
- End of week word count: 15,990.

WEEK 20

Day 1
Commitment

- Check in with your 3 people.

Days 2-7

Writing And The Upcoming One-Quarter Twist

- Average 533 words per day for at least 5 days.

Your One-Quarter Twist should occur between 18,000 and 22,000 words for an 80,000 word novel.

- End of week word count: 18,655.

21

WEEK 21

Days 1-7
Writing The One-Quarter Twist

- Average 533 words per day for at least 5 days.

If you figured out your One-Quarter Twist in advance, this session should be pretty easy. You know what needs to happen, and it's dramatic and intriguing.

Have fun!

- End of week word count: 21,320.

22

WEEK 22

Days 1-7
Moving On

- Average 533 words per day for at least 5 days.

Your protagonist is reeling from the twist at the one-quarter point. Be sure you show the emotions that raises.

- End of week word count: 23,985.

23
WEEK 23

Days 1-2
Characters and Conflict

- Do you feel that your characters fit your story?
- Is there enough conflict?
- Make a few notes on what you may want to change, but don't go back.

Days 3-7

Writing

- Average 533 words per day.
- End of week word count: 26,650.

WEEK 24

Day 1
Commitment

- You're still checking in with your 3 people, right? Let them know how it's going.

Days 2-7

Writing

- Average 533 words per day for at least 5 days.

Think about the backstory your reader will

need, meaning whatever happened before your novel began that your reader must know to understand your characters' actions and the events of the story. Most of it should be woven in during the first one-third to one-half of the book, though you may have some moments later on where you add a line or two as needed.

- What else will your reader need to know for your story to be the most compelling?
- If you haven't covered all the necessary backstory yet, think about where you'll fit it in.
- End of week word count: 29,315.

25

WEEK 25

Days 1-7
Writing Toward The Mid-Point

- Average 533 words per day for at least 5 days.

You've got about 10,000 words until the halfway mark, or Mid-Point, in your novel. (See Part 1 Week 6 for more on the Mid-Point.)

- Think about what needs to happen to get to that throw-caution-to-the-wind moment.

- You can also further develop your subplots between this point and your Mid-Point.
- End of week word count: 31,980.

WEEK 26

Days 1-7
Writing And Character Arcs

Your main characters should grow and change throughout the book. If the protagonist and antagonist are the same from beginning to end, your story will be less compelling.

- In what way do you expect your protagonist to grow and change throughout the novel?
- How about your antagonist?
- Average 533 words per day for at least 5 days.

- End of week word count: 34,645.

WEEK 27

Days 1-7
Writing Break/Think Ahead

Use this week to catch up if you've gotten behind on word count.

If you're on track and you see busy times ahead when you'll need to skip a week, go ahead and write your 533 words a day.

- If you're right where you want to be, take a break and don't write.
- Think about what else needs to happen to reach your Mid-Point.
- Do you have enough conflict?

- If not, is your protagonist committed to the goal?
- Is the antagonist both strong and equally committed (if not more committed) to an opposing, mutually-exclusive goal?
- Have you made life hard enough for your protagonist?
- If not, think of 3 ways you can make your antagonist stronger and/or your protagonist's quest more difficult.
- End of week word count: 34,645 (same as last week).

WEEK 28

Day 1
Commitment

- Check in with your 3 people.

If you're on track or close to it, you can report that you will be half-way done with your novel within the next few weeks!

If not, don't despair.

Sometimes there are turns in life's road that send us temporarily off our writing path. Author Dean Wesley Smith calls them off-ramps.

If that's happened, take a breath and reassess. Look ahead at when you can reasonably start writing again.

- As before, don't write out what's gotten in the way or how unhappy you are, simply let your 3 people know when you expect to start again. If that's unknown, let them know you're temporarily out of commission but that you'll check in again when you're back.

Days 2-7

Writing Again

Hopefully you're back on track after the break and eager to dive in.

- Average 533 words per day for at least 5 days.
- End of week word count: 37,310.

WEEK 29

Days 1-7
Almost Half-Way There

- Average 533 words per day for at least 5 days.

You should hit your Mid-Point around 38,000-42,000 words.

- End of week word count: 39,975.

30

WEEK 30

Days 1-7

Congratulations!

- Average 533 words per day for at least 5 days and you're halfway done.

Your Mid-Point should have occurred or will in the next week or so.

The half-way mark should be the most dramatic point in your story save for the Climax. It's where your protagonist takes a stand.

Make the most of it!

- End of week word count: 42,640.

WEEK 31

Day 1
Commitment

You are doing great. You're in the second half of the novel, so you can see the end of the line.

- Close your eyes and imagine the moment you finish.

If you like to type *The End*, see those words on the screen. If, like me, you like to print out your manuscript to review, envision the printer shooting out the pages. Get in touch with the sense of accomplishment you'll feel.

Days 2-7

Writing

- Average 533 words per day for at least 5 days.
- End of week word count: 45,305.

32

WEEK 32

Day 1
Commitment

- Check in with your 3 people.

Days 2-7

Writing And What's Next

- Average 533 words per day for at least 5 days.

Your protagonist should be active from your halfway point through the end—making choices and taking action based on the vow at the Mid-Point.

- If your protagonist is still mainly reacting to what others are doing or to circumstances without taking the driver's seat, make sure the Mid-Point commitment is strong enough.

Being active doesn't mean your protagonist always must be physically active or crusading or pounding the table. But your protagonist must be doing the best and most she can within the confines of who she is to move forward, pursue her goal, and prevail over the antagonist.

- End of week word count: 47,970.

WEEK 33

Days 1-7
Writing And Character Arcs

- Average 533 words per day for at least 5 days.

In Week 26 we talked about character arcs.

- How has your protagonist grown?
- Have you shown that to your readers?
- If not, think about what you might add going forward that makes that growth clear.

- End of week word count: 50,635.

WEEK 34

Days 1-7
More Writing And Character Arcs

- Average 533 words per day for at least 5 days.

Now let's talk about your antagonist.

- How has your antagonist grown?
- Have you shown that to your readers?
- If not, think about what you might add going forward that makes that growth clear.

- End of week word count: 53,300.

WEEK 35

Days 1-7
Writing

- Average 533 words per day for at least 5 days.

While you're not quite there, it's not too early to think about your upcoming Three-Quarter Turn and Climax. (See Part 1 Weeks 7 and 8 for more on the Three-Quarter Turn and the Climax.)

- If you planned those plot turns

already, adjust them if your story took an unexpected direction.
- If you didn't plan them, now's the time to consider what that last major turn will be and how your story will resolve.
- End of week word count: 55,965.

36

WEEK 36

Day 1
Commitment

- Thank your 3 people for hanging in there with you. Let them know how much it means to you.

Days 2-7

Take A Break/Catch Up

You are in the home stretch!

- Use this week to catch up if you've gotten behind, to work ahead if

you're expecting a challenging schedule in the near future, or to take a break and focus completely on the other parts of your life.
- End of week word count: 55,965 (same as last week).

WEEK 37

Days 1-7
Subplots And Writing Toward That Three-Quarter Turn

- Average 533 words per day for at least 5 days.

Your Three-Quarter Turn should occur somewhere between 58,000 and 62,000 words.

- Think about your subplots.
- How does each resolve?

- What needs to happen so that occurs?
- End of week word count: 58,630.

WEEK 38

Days 1-7
Writing The Three-Quarter Turn

- Average 533 words per day for at least 5 days.
- Write your Three-Quarter Turn if you haven't already.

It grows from your protagonist's decision at the Mid-Point. It takes your story in a new direction that drives toward the Climax.

- End of week word count: 61,295.

WEEK 39

Day 1
Commitment

You're nearing the finish line!

- Tell a friend about the reward you planned for yourself (back in Week 6—remember Week 6? You've come a long way since then).

Days 2-7

Writing From The Three-Quarter Turn Forward

- Average 533 words per day for at least 5 days.

The last quarter of the novel is typically the fastest moving.

From here on, your writing should be almost all action. Any backstory or character development should already have taken place.

All you need from now on is to write whatever it takes to get to the resolution and to tie up loose ends.

- If you find you've failed to include backstory that requires more than a line or so of explanation, note what's missing and you can weave it in when you make changes in Week 49.
- End of week word count: 63,960.

WEEK 40

Day 1
Commitment

- Share with your 3 people in a sentence how pleased, excited, and/or happy you are that you've reached this stage.

Days 2-7

Writing

- Average 533 words per day for at least 5 days.
- End of week word count: 66,625.

WEEK 41

Days 1-7
So Close To The End

- Average 533 words per day for at least 5 days.
- Figure out if the resolution of your subplot(s) should occur before or after the Climax of your main plot.
- Start setting the stage for the Climax.
- Think ahead to when you finish your novel. If you plan to send it to beta readers (one or more people you trust to give honest comments

from a reader's perspective), a story editor, and/or copy editors and proofreaders, start researching, getting recommendations from other writers, and contacting people now. They often need to know 10-12 weeks in advance to fit reviewing your novel into their schedule.
- End of week word count: 69,290.

WEEK 42

Days 1-7
Only 10% Left

- Average 533 words per day for at least 5 days.

Your main story arc is nearing the Climax.

- Enjoy writing the culmination of all your hard work.
- If you find yourself wracked with doubt about whether the plot is working, first, recognize that's

perfectly normal. Everyone feels that way!
- If you are really concerned, look at your plot turns and note ways you might adjust them, then keep writing from this point forward. If it makes you feel better, include a few notes in brackets about what worries you so you can come back to them later in our last few weeks.
- End of week word count: 71,955.

43

WEEK 43

Days 1-7

This Is It: The Climax

- Average 533 words per day for at least 5 days.

The Climax should occur somewhere between this week and your last few pages.

- This is the big payoff for your reader, so while the Climax should be fast-moving, be sure to include enough detail and depth so that your reader feels satisfied.

- End of week word count: 74,620.

WEEK 44

Day 1
Commitment

- Update your 3 people. Even if you're a little behind, you'll be able to tell them you're nearly finished.

Days 2-7

Almost There

- Average 533 words per day for at least 5 days.
- If you haven't already, wind up your plot and subplot(s).

- Finish your character arcs.
- End of week word count: 77,285.

WEEK 45

Days 1-7
Falling Action

- Average 533 words per day for at least 5 days.
- Tie up loose ends and show what the characters do, say, and feel after the Climax.
- Give a glimpse of the future.
- End of week word count: 79,950.

46
WEEK 46

ay 1
The End

- Last Words

You've finished with your first draft or are all of 50 words short if you are a rigid adherent to schedules.

- Final word count: 80,000. (Congratulations!)

Days 2-7

Catch Up/Break

- If you need to, use the rest of the week to catch up.
- Otherwise, set aside your novel. Do your best not to think of it.

WEEK 47

Days 1-7
Take A Break

Yep, that's it.

PART THREE: THE CLEAN UP PASS

WEEK 48

Day 1
Commitment

You've finished a rough draft, and with a little clean up you'll have a solid draft you're ready to share.

- Tell your 3 people the good news.

Days 2-7

Read Through For The Big Picture

- Read through your manuscript. Ideally, do this in print, as it's easier

to view the book objectively when you see it on paper.
- Write notes to yourself either in the margins or in a separate document about major points to change. Highlight/include any notes you typed into the manuscript as you went along about edits or concerns.

Major points can include:

- Adjusting the actions or motivations of your main characters (including choosing different goals for the protagonist or antagonist)
- Rearranging, adding, or deleting scenes to keep the story moving and the plot turns occurring roughly at the one-quarter, one-half, and three-quarter points
- Changing the plot turns entirely
- Changing the overall point-of-view
- Significantly altering the plot or characters in some other way

If you planned your story before writing, you probably won't need to make too many of these types of changes.

If you skipped right to the writing phase, you may need to make more major changes, so you'll use those 11 planning weeks you skipped in the beginning now.

WEEK 49

Days 1-7
Changes To Plots And Subplots

- Make the changes you marked last week that affect your plots and subplots. (Don't worry if you have quite a few, you'll have next week to finish them.)
- If your characters' goals changed, that affects the plot and is included this week (and next), as it will almost always require adjusting your major plot turns.
- If you decided to change the overall

point of view (for instance, switching from first person to limited third person), write any additional scenes or revised scenes from the new point of view.

WEEK 50

Days 1-7
Plot And Story Changes Continued

- Finish your plot and subplot adjustments.
- If you didn't need to make many changes, start on the remaining issues you flagged in Week 48.

WEEK 51

Days 1-7
Character And Point Of View Changes

- Make any remaining adjustments and edits, including addressing character issues and ensuring your point of view is consistent throughout the novel.

52

WEEK 52

Days 1-6
Last Of The Clean Up

- Make any last edits.

Day 7

Commitment And Celebration

- Tell your 3 people you've finished a solid first draft of your novel! Thank them again for their support.
- Celebrate, claim your reward from Week 6, tell your friends and family,

and take some time away to enjoy (non-writing) life.

You did it!

53

WHAT'S NEXT?

What do you do with your first draft?

Some writers send the manuscript to a developmental editor (also called a story editor) to get feedback on the plot and characters before devoting more time to revising. Others send their book to beta readers for the same type of feedback.

Still others let the manuscript sit for a few weeks first and do their own scene-level rewrite before sharing it with anyone else. (That's what I do now. With my first few novels I sought feedback on my first draft.)

If you want to do a scene-level revision, ask yourself at least these questions:

- Is each scene necessary to a plot or subplot?
- Is the point of view the strongest choice for each scene? And does the viewpoint character have the most at stake in that scene?
- Does the writing bring your reader into each scene using all five senses, not only sight and hearing?
- Are the characters' emotions and motives clear enough for the reader to understand?
- Are your characters behaving in ways your reader will believe?

Allow 2 months for the revision process. That time frame builds in 2-3 weeks for you to let the manuscript sit and/or for others to comment, 2-3 weeks for you to revise at the scene level, and 2-4 weeks for you to review again and make any last changes.

You may be able to work faster than that, but it's better to build in extra time and be pleasantly surprised if you finish early.

Seeking Feedback

There's a lot of advice out there about whether to seek comments from beta readers and/or a professional story editor before publishing your novel or querying agents or traditional publishers.

Critics of using beta readers and story editors argue that it shows a lack of confidence in the writer's own vision and craft and that too many cooks spoils the broth.

There's something to that. Sending your work to 5 or 10 (or 20) people and trying to respond to all the concerns they raise will likely make your novel a hodgepodge that will please no one.

Also, it's tricky if you ask other writers for feedback because it's hard for any writer to resist saying what she would do with the story rather than commenting on what's on the page.

My own view is that it's helpful to get feedback from someone you feel confident will tell you what's **not** working (pats on the back are nice, but are no help if you want to improve your novel) in a useful way and who loves the type of novel you write. (Comments from a huge fan of literary fiction who dislikes commercial work probably won't help if you write fast-paced thrillers and vice versa. In fact, that feedback might damage your writing, as the pacing can be radically different in those two types of books.)

If you find a trusted reader who loves what you love, that person's notes on when the story feels slow, the characters' actions aren't believable, or it's not clear what's happening, can be very useful.

Before You Publish Or Submit

What everyone agrees on is that before you publish or submit your manuscript to an agent or publishing house, you need to copyedit and proofread it. You can hire a professional editor or proofreader, learn to do it yourself, or trade services with other writers. If you trade services or hire a professional, be sure that person is good at what they do. Ask them to review and edit a sample for you. (I've seen poorly-edited books filled with typos where the author paid a "professional" copy editor.)

Whatever route you take, I recommend **Self Editing for Fiction Writers** by Renni Browne and Dave King. Even if you plan to hire someone, this book will help you determine if that person did a good job.

Also, the article **7 Tips For Proofreading Your Novel** on WritingAsASecondCareer.com has advice for improving the likelihood of catching errors in your own work.

Allow an additional 2-3 weeks for copy-editing and proofreading if you do it yourself.

You'll need time for the following tasks:

- Let the manuscript sit a few days to view it with fresh eyes
- Read it carefully in small chunks (ideally no more than 5-10 pages at a time)
- Type in the changes
- Compare the corrected pages to the edits you marked

If you hire someone, the turnaround time will depend on that person's schedule. Allow yourself 3-4 days to review and input that person's changes.

Other Resources

If you'd like to read more about plot or about character development, check out my books **Super Simple Story Structure: A Quick Guide To Plotting And Writing Your Novel; Buffy And The Art Of Story Season One: Writing Better Fiction By Watching Buffy;** and **Creating Compelling Characters From The Inside Out** or listen to my podcast **Buffy and the Art of Story.**

I also offer individual feedback on your novel's plot and personal story coaching. Or, for those who prefer online self-study courses, I created **How To Plot Your Novel: From Idea To First Draft.** You can find out more at Help With Your Novel on the website WritingAsASecondCareer.com.

Good luck!

The One-Year Novelist

Did you enjoy this book and find it helpful?
Please write a review to help others find out about it. Even a sentence or a few words can make a difference.

ABOUT THE AUTHOR

An author, lawyer, and adjunct professor of law, L. M. Lilly's non-fiction includes *Happiness, Anxiety, and Writing: Using Your Creativity To Live A Calmer, Happier Life; Super Simple Story Structure: A Quick Guide to Plotting & Writing Your Novel; Buffy And The Art Of Story Season One: Writing Better Fiction By Watching Buffy*; and *Creating Compelling Characters From The Inside Out*.

Writing as Lisa M. Lilly, she is the author of the bestselling Awakening supernatural thriller series about Tara Spencer, a young woman who becomes the focus of a powerful religious cult when she mysteriously finds herself pregnant, and of the Q.C. Davis mystery series, a traditional detective series set in Lilly's hometown of Chicago. She is currently working on the latest book in that series.

Lilly also is the author of **When Darkness Falls**, a gothic horror novel set in Chicago's South Loop, and the short-story collection **The Tower Formerly Known as Sears and Two Other Tales of Urban Horror**, the title story of which was made into the short film Willis Tower.

She is the host of the podcast **Buffy and the Art of Story**.

ALSO BY L. M. LILLY

Super Simple Story Structure: A Quick Guide to Plotting and Writing Your Novel

Creating Compelling Characters From The Inside Out

Write On: How To Overcome Writer's Block So You Can Write Your Novel

Happiness, Anxiety, and Writing: Using Your Creativity To Live A Calmer, Happier Life

Buffy And The Art Of Story Season One: Writing Better Fiction By Watching Buffy

Buffy And The Art Of Story Season Two Part 1

Buffy And The Art Of Story Season Two Part 2

How To Write A Novel, Grades 6-8

As Lisa M. Lilly:

The Awakening (Book 1 in The Awakening Series)

The Unbelievers (Book 2 in The Awakening Series)

The Conflagration (Book 3 in The Awakening Series)

The Illumination (Book 4 in The Awakening Series)

The Complete Awakening Supernatural Thriller Series Box Set

When Darkness Falls (a standalone supernatural suspense novel)

The Tower Formerly Known As Sears And Two Other Tales Of Urban Horror

The Worried Man (Q.C. Davis Mystery 1)

The Charming Man (Q.C. Davis Mystery 2)

The Fractured Man (Q.C. Davis Mystery 3)

The Troubled Man (Q.C. Davis Mystery 4)

The Hidden Man (Q.C. Davis Mystery 5)

Q.C. Davis Mysteries 1-3 (The Worried Man, The Charming Man, and The Fractured Man) Box Set

www.ingramcontent.com/pod-product-compliance
Lightning Source LLC
Chambersburg PA
CBHW050326120526
44592CB00014B/2072